A Boy Named Jack

A storybook series

Book seven:

A Baker in the Making

Written by Quay Roads

Visit the author's website at www.ABoyNamedJack.us
Illustrated by Valentina Valenza

ISBN-13: 978-0998715377
ISBN-10: 0998715379

Library of Congress Control Number: 2018956953

Printed in the United States of America

Dedication

These books are always dedicated to my children and husband who constantly support me and let me be me. This time I especially want to thank my friends at Dragonflies and Fairytales Daycare, who are always my champions and have helped me realize my dream of creating Jack.

~Quay Roads

Introduction

My family homesteaded in New Mexico over 100 years ago, back in the days of cowboys and covered wagons. My brother and I were raised on a ranch not far from the homes where both of our parents grew up. Rural, ranch life was not glamorous but it was warm and wonderful, full of experiences unique to that time and place. It is my hope to bring to life some of the everyday adventures my brother and I had and share them with you and your children.

Table of Contents

1

Pookie

This is Mom's story.

Dad has his horses.

Jack has Rusty.

Alice has Samantha and her other cats.

Mom has two little dogs, Taffy and Scooter.

Taffy and Scooter are loveable, long dogs with short legs called dachshunds.

Some people call them wiener dogs because they look like hot dogs.

Taffy is black with brown markings and has long hair.

Scooter is red and very beautiful.

Their legs are very short.

They cannot jump on the chair.

Mom has to pick them up so they can be on the couch.

They love to sit on Mom's lap and get some good loving scratches when Mom is relaxing.

Mom is happy to learn that Taffy and Scooter are going to be parents.

Taffy is going to be a momma!

In just a few weeks, Taffy has three puppies.

They are little red puppies.

Little red puppies with big brown eyes.

They look just like their daddy, Scooter.

Taffy snuggles and loves on her little puppies.

Mom has decided to name the smallest one Pookie.

The other puppies get names, too.

The girl is named Molly and the boy is named Tex.

Alice wanted to name them Rubish and Mallarky but Mom said "no".

So the puppies are Pookie, Molly and Tex.

As the puppies grow, they learn to run and to play.

Pookie and her siblings also learn to sit up on their bottoms and beg.

It is very cute to see Taffy, Scooter, and three little puppies sit up.

Alice puts a red scarf around Pookie's neck.

Molly gets a sparkly pink collar.

Tex has a collar from braided leather that Dad made.

Pookie and her siblings have toys but their favorite toy to play with is a toy fox.

It has a squeaker inside its nose and the puppies bite it to make the fox squeak.

They shake the little fox and growl like they are such big tough dogs.

Squeak! Squeak!

All through the house, the little fox squeaks as the rowdy little puppies bite and pull and shake the toy.

2

A Baker in the Making

This is Alice's story.

Mom is a good baker.

Mom makes wonderful cakes from scratch.

This means she follows a recipe and mixes all the ingredients together to make her cakes.

Mom has a big notebook full of recipes she has added to since she was a schoolgirl.

Alice thinks that was a very long time ago!

Mom is teaching Alice how to cook.

Alice loves to bake cakes, too.

Alice has a little pink oven that bakes little cakes.

Alice's cakes are from a mix.

This means she just adds some milk to the special dry ingredients that are in the packet.

Alice mixes the batter together and pours it into the small cake pan.

Then Alice slides the pan into her little oven.

The lightbulb inside her oven gets warm enough to bake her little cake.

In 15 minutes, Alice has a nice, warm little cake.

Today Alice has made a cake for the mailman.

Alice thinks the mailman is very nice.

Alice had her little cake wrapped on a plate so the mailman could take it with him as he delivered more mail.

The mailman told Mom and Alice he was happy with his little cake.

Last week Alice stayed after school with some friends, Kimberly and Liberty.

Their mother was making a cake so she let the girls help.

They turned on the radio and started dancing while baking the cake.

The girls made a mess by throwing powdered sugar and flour at each other.

Soon there was white powder in their hair.

There was white powder on the floor and on the walls.

There was white powder all over everyone in the room!

What a sweet, sticky mess!

3

The Old House

Mom and Dad used to live at a very small, old house down the road.

Sometimes they all go visit the old house.

This old house in the country has peacocks.

Peacocks are beautiful, big birds.

Every morning the peacocks make their call to each other.

"Ahhhh whaaahhhh, ahhhh whaaahhhh", the peacocks cry.

They are noisy, but Alice thinks peacocks are beautiful.

She likes to pick up the feathers they have lost and see all the colors.

At this old house there is an old garage.

Alice is afraid to go near the garage.

Dad told her there are bats in the garage.

The bats hang upside down from the ceiling.

There is also an old outhouse near the garage.

An outhouse can be used in the winter when the pipes freeze in the house and you can't use the bathroom.

Alice NEVER goes by the outhouse.

Alice thinks it is scary and stinky!

One day when they were visiting the old house, Mom could not find Jack.

Mom looked everywhere and called for Jack.

Still, Mom could not find Jack.

Mom ran around the corner of the house and could see Jack.

Jack was wearing a bright blue sweater.

Jack's sweater got caught in the barbed wire fence.

Jack was stuck in the fence!

Jack was crying so hard because he was stuck in the fence and could not get out.

Mom helped Jack get unstuck from the fence.

Last time Jack got stuck in the fence, he got a big scratch on his head.

The scratch left a scar and now the hair does not grow there.

Jack looks like he has a part in his hair from the big scratch.

Maybe Jack should just stay away from the fences!

4

The Party Line

Now that Alice is older, Mom and Dad teach her to answer the telephone.

Jack already knows how to answer the phone and how to make a phone call.

The phone in Mom's house has buttons to push for each number.

The phone in Grandma's house is older and is called a rotary phone.

There is a big circle with numbers around it and you have to put your finger in the hole next to the number you want and make it go around.

Some phones in the country are special.

They use party lines.

This means that more than one family uses the same phone line.

Mom and Dad's phone line is shared by four other homes nearby.

When you pick up the phone to make a call, you must first listen to see if someone else is already using the phone.

If someone is already talking you must hang up right away.

You must never listen in to their conversation.

Jack and Alice are allowed to answer the phone.

They must be very polite when they answer the phone.

If Mom and Dad are not in the house, Jack and Alice must write down who called.

They must take a message for Mom and Dad.

Answering the telephone is a very big responsibility for Alice and she is proud of herself.

<u>5</u>

Paper Dolls

This is Alice's story.

Yesterday Mom visited Grandmommy at her big house.

Mom brought home a box.

Mom said it was a very special box.

Alice could see it was an old box.

Mom carries the box and holds Alice's hand as they sit in the middle of the floor.

Mom tells Alice a very important part of her childhood is in this box.

Alice is full of anticipation.

Mom slowly lifts the lid off the box.

Alice can see layers and layers of colorful papers.

Very carefully Mom lifts out the papers.

They are pretty cut-outs of little girls and women.

"These are my old paper dolls", says Mom.

"When I was a little girl, I spent hours playing with my paper dolls".

Mom says that famous ladies had their images made into paper dolls and shows Alice her dolls of movie stars like Janet Leigh and Jane Powell.

The box is also full of colorful dresses and other outfits and accessories for the dolls.

Each piece of clothing as tabs around the edges so they attach to the paper doll.

There are even little purses and scarves for them!

Mom says she used to make furniture and beds for her dolls out of tissue boxes and other little boxes.

Mom also used to cut out pretty dresses for her dolls from catalogs and magazines.

She just had to look for the catalog models to be similar to her paper doll ladies.

Alice sat in wonder and looked at all the fragile dolls and their clothing.

Mom's old paper dolls are amazing treasures and Alice is very careful with them.

6

Alice's Beautiful Necklace

It is time for school pictures.

Mom has picked out nice clothes for Jack and Alice to wear.

Alice will be wearing a pretty pink dress.

Jack has a nice new shirt to wear in his pictures.

Alice also has a necklace.

Alice thinks this necklace is beautiful.

It has blue and white beads.

Alice loves her necklace and wants to wear it in her school picture.

Mom does not want Alice to wear the necklace.

Mom does not think Alice's necklace is beautiful.

Alice sneaks the necklace in her school bag.

Alice takes her necklace to school on picture day.

Alice thinks she will put the necklace on and have it under her collar.

Alice thinks even if the necklace does not show in the picture she will like that she had it on.

On picture day, Alice takes her necklace to school and puts it on when she brushes her hair.

She tucks it under her dress collar.

No one will ever know.

Mom will never know that Alice wore the necklace on picture day!

Except that when the pictures come in, the necklace shows!

One side of Alice's collar was turned up and there is the necklace.

There is the blue and white beaded necklace!

Alice was in trouble again!!

7

Dad's Almost Pet

One late spring afternoon Dad was headed back to the house when he saw something interesting on the side of the road.

He stopped the truck and saw a skunk family.

There was the bigger momma skunk in front and 6 smaller baby skunks following in a line.

Skunks look a little bit like black and white cats, with fuzzy tails.

They all walked slowly down the bar ditch on the side of the road.

Dad was careful to stay quiet and not scare the skunks.

Dad was also careful to keep the window rolled up because skunks stink, especially if they get scared.

Skunks spray an awful stink when they get scared and no one wants to be around that!

Still Dad was very interested in the baby skunks.

The last baby skunk in line was pure white.

Dad thought a pet skunk would be an amazing pet.

A white pet skunk would be so unusual.

Alice would probably love to snuggle one of these babies.

Their hair looks soft, almost like a cat's hair.

Unfortunately, skunks do not smell like cats.

Dad knew the momma skunk would not just let him take one of her babies.

Dad also knew Mom would not be happy about having a stinky skunk in her house!

Dad let the momma skunk and her babies wander off down the road.

That is how the white baby skunk ended up being the almost pet.

About the Author

Quay Roads grew up on a ranch in rural New Mexico with her parents and older brother. Jack's adventures are taken from her experiences growing up in the country and mixed in with some funny stories from her own children. Quay Roads now lives in Florida and enjoys spending time with her husband, 3 adult children and 1 grandson who has endless energy and hugs.

More in the Jack series

Thank you for spending time with Jack and his family and for enjoying his adventures. I hope you are having fun. Please go to www.ABoyNamedJack.us to learn more about the other books in the A Boy Named Jack: a storybook series.

www.ingramcontent.com/pod-product-compliance
Lightning Source LLC
Chambersburg PA
CBHW041806040426
42448CB00005B/291

I0161751

Paperback ISBN: 978-1-0689035-3-3

Disclaimer: The dream told in this book is an original parable to help explain the gospel. The Scriptures located at the bottom of many of the pages are examples of Bible verses that could apply, not an exhaustive list.

Jenny Alexander Publishing

I was floundering in the sea.
I needed someone to save me.

With my arms flailing about,
I began to loudly shout.

I shouted so much, I lost my voice. Didn't I have another choice?

Apparently not. There was no one else around. Aside from seagulls and waves, there was no other sound.

WHERE IS EVERYBODY?

But a still small voice spoke deep inside. It said, "Call out to Jesus. There is no need to hide."

Romans 10:13

Since there was no other way, I hesitated not. "Jesus help," I ever so quietly said. At once, a life jacket went over my head.

Before I knew it, I was safely ashore. I was so exhausted, I fell asleep and began to snore.

When I awoke, I realized I'd dreamed. And then I remembered, I'd been redeemed.

Galatians 3:13

In real life, Jesus was like a life vest to me. He saved me from darkness, gave me rest, set me free.

Colossians 1:13, 14
Matthew 11:28-30

I was guilty of sin, but He paid the price. His sacrifice was way more than just nice.

I LIED. I DISOBEYED MOM AND DAD. I SAID BAD THINGS ABOUT MY FRIEND.

2 Corinthians 5:21

He loved me so much He cleared my name. Though I'd done wrong, He took the blame.

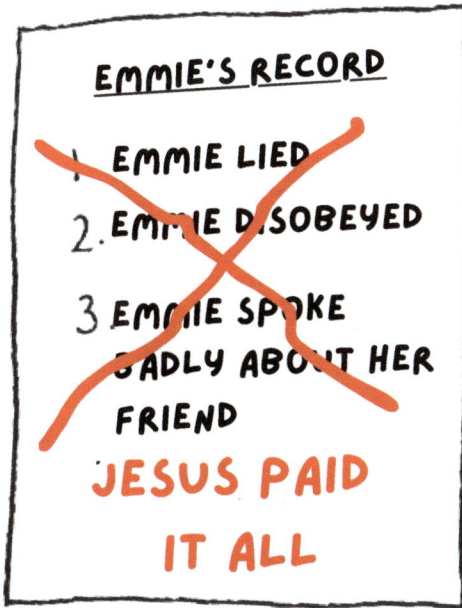

EMMIE'S RECORD

1. EMMIE LIED
2. EMMIE DISOBEYED
3 EMMIE SPOKE BADLY ABOUT HER FRIEND

JESUS PAID IT ALL

Romans 3:23-25

He died on the cruel cross.
My amazing gain was His loss.

Galatians 3:13

I'm now safe as safe can be.
Thanks to His work at Calvary.

John 5:24
John 10:28

What's true for me can be for you. Believe on His name. That's all you must do.

Believe

He did the work, He did it all. He undid mankind's fall.

Genesis 3
1 Corinthians 15:22

Why not allow Him to be your life vest? Trust him only. He did the rest.

Then you can join me and be safe in His arms. Less likely to be led astray by the world's charms.

1 Timothy 6:10
1 John 2:15

I hope to see you on the other side. Where His arms will be open wide.

They'll be open wide for me and for you. Because we trusted His work, not ours. There's no need to doubt, it's true.

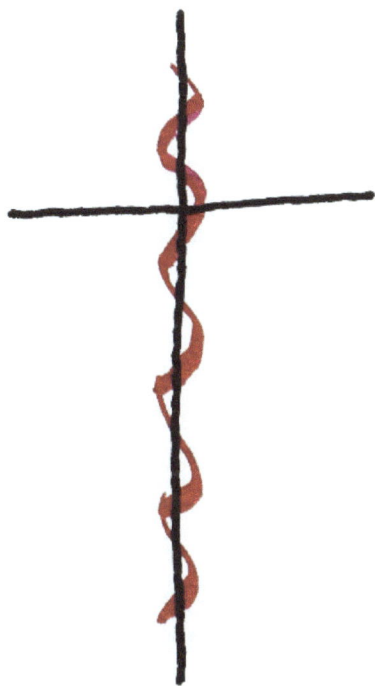

2 Corinthians 5:6,8

So, put your mind to rest.
Consider it done. Your salvation
has been purchased by Jesus,
the One.

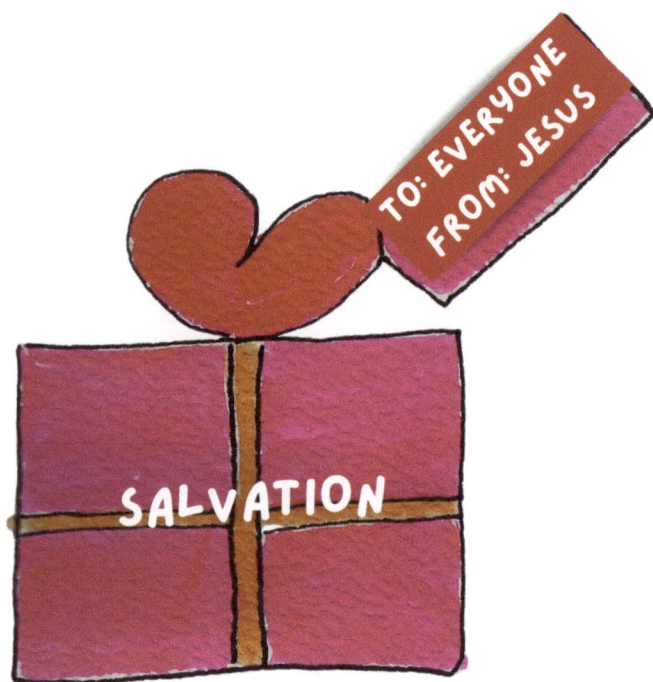

TO: EVERYONE
FROM: JESUS

SALVATION

Ephesians 2:8–9

There's no need to wander and flounder about. There's no need to go through life full of doubt.

WHY AM I WANDERING? JESUS IS THE WAY!

John 14:6

Jesus is like a life vest. We need only grab on. Like so many others before us have done.

Hebrews 12:1

Every human being has the same choice. It's why I'm writing this book and using my voice.

Will you trust in Jesus' finished work?

YES

OR

NO

2 Corinthians 5:20

I want others to know about
this great gift. That has been
given to repair the rift.

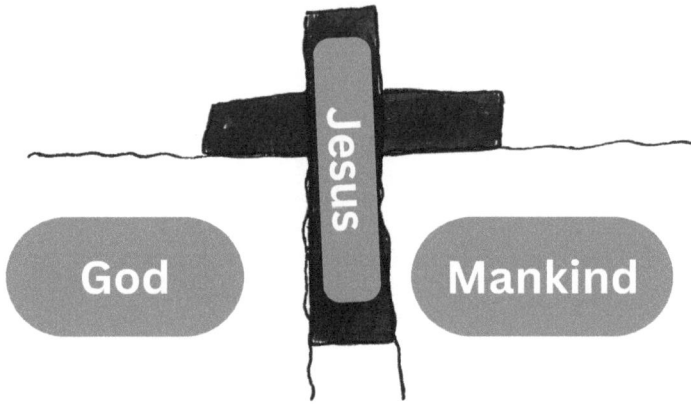

John 14:6

The rift that our sin has created with God. And the remedy that should leave us all awed.

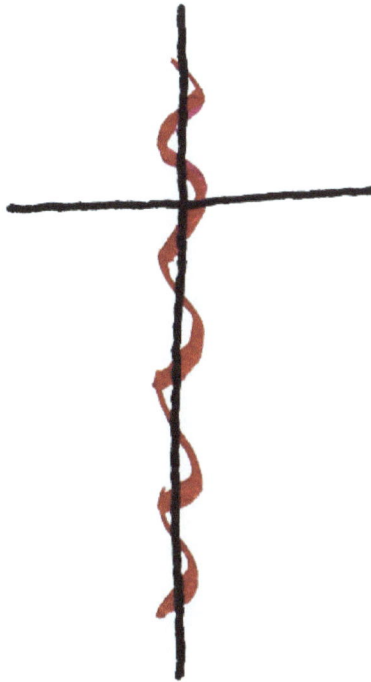

1 Peter 3:18

So, to His grace won't you say yes? His great desire is to bless.

Bless

Psalm 1
Psalm 23
Psalm 103

28

Say yes to Jesus, and you'll be made new. Just like I was, you can be too.

2 Corinthians 5:17

Trust in Jesus, hold on to His Word. Call on His name. You'll surely be heard.

John 6:37

Reflection Questions:

1. What did you learn from this book?
2. Do you still have questions about salvation? If so, you're welcome to visit knowimsaved.com. That's where I found help when I needed it.

Acknowledgments

Thank you to my husband, Curtis Alexander. Your support and input on this book were so helpful as always.

Thank you to Richard Fulton and knowimsaved.com for the spiritual help you gave me in 2019.

Review Request

Your opinion matters! Could you take a brief moment to leave a review on Amazon? Your kind feedback is super important in helping others find this book and much appreciated. Thank you so much for your time.

www.ingramcontent.com/pod-product-compliance
Lightning Source LLC
Chambersburg PA
CBHW041822040426
42448CB00025B/39